The Smile Book

By

Joann Rohrbach

This book is dedicated to all the smiles among us.

Contents

Smiles

Some smiles are silly and others, sad.
Then there's the good and also the bad.
They come in all colors and quite a sight.
Watch out for those that give us a fright.

Special ones are sweet, others seem tart.
Some make us mad and keep us apart.
There are sad, sulky, shy and slow.
They make us feel either high or low.

It's obvious some arrive with a flirt.
Watch for the stern that keep us alert.
I love the easy, gentle or sleepy.
I hate the mean, ugly and creepy.

Some smiles are bright and big as the sun.
They're also playful when we're having fun.
Some come from jokers big and wide.
Some are sneaky if there's something to hide.

Smiles make the whole world go around.
Everywhere you look they are easily found.
There's nothing like a happy smile to see.
It doesn't matter who's wearing it, you or me.

ABC's of Smiles

Apple pie
Baby's coo
Cat's meow
Dog's bow wow
Easy recipes
Funny clowns
Good friends
Happy times
I love you
Jokes to hear
Kindness to share
Love and laughter
Money honey
New shoes
Old music
Playing games
Quick chores
Roses and rainbows
Sunshine and smiles
Television shows
Umbrellas for rain
Victorious wins
World Wide Web
Xylophones
You and me
Zip-a-Dee-Doo-Dah days

Smiles Make You Shine!

What's a smile? As if you didn't know! A smile is a facial expression characterized by an upward curving of the corners of your mouth and indicating pleasure, amusement, or disdain. It's a pleasant or favorable disposition or aspect. A smile is to beam or grin.

Did you ever notice how a smile affects people? No matter where we are, to see a smile makes us feel good. And more often than not, no matter what kind of mood we are in, we smile back automatically.

A smile can mean so many things. It means you like, approve or accept someone. It means you understand and/or love someone. It means you are warm, accepting and open to communication. It can also be a polite way to acknowledge another person without having to become involved in a conversation with them. Of course that can work in reverse. There are lewd and rude smiles too. Don't you just hate those?

I'm a people watcher. Are you? Like when we are sitting in the doctor's office, waiting for our turn which seems to take forever. It's a nice diversion to keep your mind occupied somehow. If you watch people coming and going, you will notice how they enter the room affects everyone there. Are they happy or sad?

To see a grumpy person with a scowl on their face makes us a little edgy. Someone who acts better than everyone else makes us feel sort of perturbed. A rude person makes us uncomfortable. To see someone smile and politely offer a hello makes us want to respond in kind. It's one thing to interact this way with strangers. But the ones who reap the most benefit from our smiles are those closest to us, such as our family and friends. We should never underestimate a smile.

Sometimes we don't realize how our demeanor affects others, especially our smiles. Our body language gives off messages to others that we're probably not even aware of. Strangers will react to us one way, yet those closest to us quite another. That's because we are creatures of habit and it is expected behavior on our part. We all can and should smile more!

If we don't smile much and started smiling more all of a sudden, others would think we are up to something. Often, they will be on the defensive before you even open your mouth, depending on what your normal temperament is. It's all in your body language.

People who don't smile much are often avoided even when they are really nice people. They might be sad, lonely, bored, tired or upset over something. We don't always feel like smiling!

We can attract more flies with honey than vinegar. It's the same with people. We should consider very seriously just how far a warm and friendly smile goes. So open up and let the sunshine in. Smile and the whole world might smile with you!

Smiles and Laughter

Laughter, the best medicine, always starts with a smile Have you ever noticed when some people smile a lot, they also laugh easily. Once some of us start, we can't seem to stop? We sometimes see or hear things that tickle our funny bone. We often get the giggles some kind of bad, sometimes for hours afterwards. Some of us even laugh at ourselves. I know that I do. One thing for sure, laughing never hurts, unless it's our tummy muscles from laughing too hard.

It can be embarrassing at times, especially if someone with you doesn't share your humor. They give you a look like you've lost your mind. Perhaps we haven't made a total fool of ourselves yet, but we're afraid that could happen one day.

No doubt, laughing is infectious. Oftentimes seeing someone else laugh can make us laugh even harder.

A few people get to laughing so hard, they actually wet their pants. Some sneeze and cry tears of joy all over the place. Once you know what to expect from those folks, you can kindly (or smartly) move out of the way, as they run for the restroom or grab for a tissue.

Laughter is the best medicine. Laughing is good for our health. It stimulates happy hormones in our brain and makes us feel good all over.

Everyone differs. Some have a great sense of humor and can take a joke as well as play one. The clown inside of them is automatically drawn to those who know how to joke and laugh. On the opposite side of humor, some people have no funny bone at all and are not amused at anything.

A sense of humor can be one of our best attributes, and attracts other people to us for obvious reasons. More often than not, a great sense of humor makes a personality shine.

Joking, playing around, teasing and laughing, often runs in families. We can sometimes recall a humorous situation from the past that can keep us laughing for years. Many of our warmest recollections were shared inside our very own family.

There are many great comedians that tickle our funny bones. When we listen to them, we can't stop laughing. That's why comedy clubs are popping up all over the place. Reading humor books and watching comedy on television or at the movie theatre also helps to relieve stress. It's good to lighten up sometimes since it makes us forget our problems, even if only for a short while.

If you too get carried away laughing, be on the safe side. Make sure you are sitting firmly on a towel to soak up wet spots. Have plenty of tissues handy to clean up sneezes and tears of joy.

Is the ability to laugh a blessing or a curse? The

answer is obvious. Have you ever wondered how many millions of people are laughing right now?

Have you had your dose of laughter today? You can always find a good laugh if you learn to laugh at yourself. Even if all you can manage is a smile, it's a good thing because it can lead to laughing. Relax, smile, and laugh a little. You will be delighted to find how good it makes you, and those around you, feel.

Smile Quotations

A Smile costs nothing but gives much. It enriches those who receive without making poorer those who give. It takes but a moment, but the memory of it sometimes lasts forever. None is so rich or mighty that he cannot get along without it and none is so poor that he cannot be made rich by it. Yet a smile cannot be bought, begged, borrowed, or stolen, for it is something that is of no value to anyone until it is given away. Some people are too tired to give you a smile. Give them one of yours, as none needs a smile as much as he who has no more to give.
–Author Unknown

The world always looks brighter from behind a smile.
–Author Unknown

If you smile at someone, they might smile back.
–Author Unknown

Wear a smile, one size fits all.
–Unknown Author

Peace begins with a smile.
–Mother Teresa

Smile, it's only a movie!
–Author Joann Rohrbach

Emoticons

If you're new to the Internet, you might be confused seeing messages containing odd-looking words and punctuation known as emoticons or smileys. If you've been around the Internet for a time, then you're probably used to seeing some of them.

I don't use them often, but wonder what they mean when someone else uses them in communicating with me.

They are not a bad thing and can be great fun. However, sometimes it seems as if they are taking over. There's so many new ones added every day, it's easy to get lost among them.

Emoticons are cyber-language, representations of smiles, frowns, etc. Emoticons are often called Internet shorthand. They are emotion icons used to replace facial expressions you would normally use when talking face to face with someone. The list has grown over the years to include more than we would ever use.

Emoticons are a very clever use of standard punctuation marks to express a human emotion. Suppose you're typing a statement such as:
I'm feeling happy!

In order to inflect your mood, your sentence looks like this with a smile added: I'm feeling happy:)

Emoticons (emotional icons) are used to compensate for the inability to convey voice inflections, facial expressions, and bodily gestures in written communication.

Emoticons can be very effective toward avoiding misinterpretation of the writer's intent. There are no standard definitions for emoticons. Most emoticons will look like a face (eyes, nose, and mouth) when rotated 90 degrees clockwise.

Aside from the commonly used ones, they are unlike the abbreviated form of acronyms and harder to figure out. For example, when you see LOL written in a sentence, you can usually figure out it's a shortened acronym for *Laughing Out Loud*.

Emoticons can be quicker than typing out a long sentence to convey your meaning when communicating with another. But if you're not up on what they mean, it can be frustrating at best for the person on the receiving end trying to research and figure out what the user meant. There are some people that love the challenge and using smileys can be lots of fun if they are up to it.

As you've seen, an emotion icon (emoticon), is a small icon composed of punctuation characters that indicates how an e-mail message should be interpreted (that is, the writer's mood). For example, a :-) emoticon indicates that the message is meant as a joke and shouldn't be taken seriously.

Your basic smiley is used to inflect a sarcastic or joking statement since we can't hear voice inflection over email :)

Here are a few commonly used ones in cyber-space. Which ones do you recognize?

:-)
User happy, mildly sarcastic comment
:-(
Sad face
;-)
Winky face, a flirtatious remark
:->
Mean or sarcastic comment
>:-)
Grinning devil, extremely devilish comment
>;->
Winking devil, mean or evil comment
O:-)
Angelic, sweet and innocent remark
:-O
Yelling or shocked
:-I
Indifferent
:) or :-)
Happiness, sarcasm, or joke
:(or :-(
Unhappiness
:] or :-]
Jovial happiness
:[or :-[
Despondent unhappiness

14

:I or :-I
Indifference
:-/ or :-\
Undecided, confused, skeptical
:/ or :\.
Undecided, confused, skeptical
:Q or :-Q
Confusion
:S or :-S
Incoherence or loss of words
:@ or :-@
Shock or screaming
:O or :-O
Surprise, yelling, realizing an error

Here's a longer list. I hope that it helps you in finding out what you need to know. You can see how varied, original, clever and frustrating (LOL) they can be.

:-)
Joking
:-0
Bored
<G>
Grinning
;-)
Winking
:-(
Sad
:-<
Frowning
(0-0)
John Lennon

~~:-[
Net Flame
:-$
Put Your Money Where Your Mouth Is
:-P
Sticking Out Tongue
:-@
Screaming, Swearing, Angry
#-)
Oh, what a night!
:-O
Yelling, Shocked
:-|
Frowning
:*)
Drunk, Clown
=|:-)=
Abe Lincoln
>;->
Wicked Grin
:-#
Been Smacked In The Mouth, Kiss
R-)
Broken Glasses
(:-)
Bald
:-{)
Mustache
!-)
Black Eye
:-)))
Is Very Fat

:-&
Biting Tongue
:-{}
Wears Lipstick
@:-)
Wears A Turban
>:->
Leering
$-)
Just Won A Large Sum Of Money
:,(
Crying
:=)
Two Noses
8:]
Gorilla
8-)
Wears Glasses
B:-)
Wears Sun Glasses On Head
:-T
Keeping A Straight Face, Tight Lipped
:-y
Said With A Smile
:-|
Disgusted, Grim, No Expression
:~-(
Crying, Shed A Tear
:'-(
Crying
:~(~~
Crying

:-Q
A Smoker
:-!
A Smoker
%-\
Has A Hangover
|-o
Bored
:-X
A Kiss, Lips Are Sealed
(:-D
Has A Big Mouth
(:+)
Has A Big Nose
:-{)
Has A Moustache
:-*
Just Ate Something Sour, Bitter Taste
[:-)
Is Wearing A Walkman
O:-)
An Angel
*<:-)>
Santa
o-<:-{{{
Santa
*<|:-)
Santa, A Clown
5:-)
Elvis Presley
:-%
Banker

:-:
Mutant Smiley
(-:|:-)
Siamese Twins
7:-)
Fred Flintstone
C):-O
A Barbershop Quartet
3:-o
A Cow
8:-)
A Pig, A Little Girl
:V
A Woodpecker
]:->
The Devil
,-)
A One Eyed Wink
|-(
Lost Contact Lenses
#:-)
Matted Hair, Crew cut, Messy Hair
&:-)
Curly Hair
C=:-)
A Chef
><:>==
A Turkey
@}->--
A Rose
=|:-)=
Uncle Sam

:_)
A Boxer, Nose Is Sliding Of Face
>>:-)
Devil, Horrible User
>>>>>(:-)
A Hat Salesman
{
A Psycho
(:I
An Egghead
b:-)
A Baseball Fan, Has A Cap On
(-)
Needs A Haircut
;-(*)
Feels Sick
[:]
A Robot
:-[
A Vampire, Count Dracula, Pouting
:-F
Bucktoothed, Major Dental Problems
:=)
Orangutan, Has Two Noses
:-?
Smokes a Pipe
:-8(
Condescending
8-#
Death, Dead
>>:-<<
Mad

20

;^)
Smirking
>>:-1
Klingon
:-----}
Liar, Pinocchio
!-(
Black Eye
)
Cheshire Cat
(:-D
Blabber Mouth
:-'|
Has A Cold, Flu
:$)
Donald Trump
:-.)
Marilyn Monroe, Madonna
:-) 8
Dolly Parton
:-|:-|
Deja'vu
><*:oDX
A Clown
C|:-=
Charlie Chaplin
: .)
Cindy Crawford
~:o
A Baby
8(:-)
Mickey Mouse, Walt Disney

(|-| F
Robocop
3:*>
Rudolph the Reindeer
P-)
A Pirate
%-~
Picasso
':-)
Has One Eyebrow
=:-)
Cyberpunk
C:\> or D:\>
MS-DOS Programmer
>8=[...
Alien

I Can See Clearly Now ;-)
Do You? <G>

Acronyms

There's a vast amount of computer jargon used over the Internet today, especially in email and newsgroup communications. Mostly, they are a quick way to get your point across. They are also part of the emoticon family. Here are some frequently used ones. They will help you understand what others are trying to say and help you get your point across fast without mincing words.

Acronym
Interpretation

AFAICT
As far as I can tell
AFAIK
As far as I know
AFK
Away from keyboard
AIUI
As I understand it
B4
Before
BAK
Back at keyboard
BBL
Be back later
BCNU
By seeing you
BRB
Be right back

BSF
But seriously folks
BTDT
Been there, done that
BTW
By the way
BWQ
Buzz word quotient
BR
Beyond Repair
CMIIW
Correct me if I'm wrong
CUL
See you later
DYJHIW
Don't you just hate it when...
DWTH
Don't work too hard
ETLA
Extended three-letter acronym
EOF
End of file
EOL
End of lecture
F2F
Face to face
FAQ
Frequently asked questions
FHS
For Heaven's sake
FITB
Fill in the blank

FOC
Free of charge
FWIW
For what it's worth
FYE
For your entertainment
FYI
For your information
<G>
Grinning
GIGO
Garbage in garbage out
GFAL
Good for a laugh
HNSOR
Head not screwed on right
HTH
Hope this helps
IAE
In any event
ICL
In Christian love
IIRC
If I recall correctly
IME
In my experience
IMO
In my opinion
IMHO
In my humble opinion
IMNSHO
In my not so humble opinion

IOU
I owe you
IOUAA
I owe you an apology
IOUO
I owe you one
IOW
In other words
ISP
Internet service provider
ISTM
It seems to me
ISTR
I seem to recall
ITRO
In the region of...
IYSWIM
If you see what I mean
<J>
Joking
JAM
Just a minute
KISS
Keep it simple, Stupid
<L>
Laughing
L8R
Later
LMAO
Laughing my ass off
LOL
Laughing out loud (or) lots of luck

MGB
May God bless
MSU
Major screw-up
MTF
More to follow
MYOB
Mind your own business
NRN
No reply necessary
OEM
Original equipment manufacturer
OIC
Oh, I see
OTE
Over the edge
OTOH
On the other hand
OTT
Over the top
PD
Public domain
ROTFL
Rolling on the floor laughing
RSN
Real soon now
RTFP
Read the fine print
RTFAQ
Read the FAQ
<S>
Smiling

SITD
Still in the dark
SNASU
Situation normal, all screwed up
SOL
Short of luck
SUL
See you later
TC
Take care
TIA
Thanks in advance
TIC
Tongue in cheek
TLA
Three-letter acronym
TLC
Tender loving care
TOTAB
Two out of three ain't bad
TTYL
Talk to you later
TYVM
Thank you very much
WYSIWYG
What you see is what you get
<Y>
Yawning
YMMV
Your mileage may vary
BFN
Bye for now!

About the Author

Joann Rohrbach wears many talented and creative hats. She enjoys writing inspiration, poetry, fiction, and non-fiction for all ages. Joann dabbles in digital art, web page design, and music. Along with designing and making beautiful jewelry, she enjoys writing about crafts and hobbies of all kinds. Joann's art appears on her greeting cards, posters, book covers and inside her illustrated books. Other things that she enjoys are cooking, visiting interesting places, reading a good book, spending time with loved ones, collecting angels, and smiles. She brightens up the day for many who know her. More than anything, Joann loves sharing all of her creations with others. Look for more great works by Joann. Visit her website: www.sparklestar.com

About the Book

The Smile Book is a practical guide about smiles. It was written with a sense of humor, inspirational insights, and many smiles, by "The Smile Lady" herself. Through careful introspection and research, the book offers a view of the smiling universe. There's as many smiles as there are faces. So many smiles and so little time! Have you ever wondered what all those shortcut smileys mean in cyber language? You will find a helpful list included in the book that can be used as a reference guide to interpret and understand the language of emoticons and acronyms.

More books by Joann Rohrbach
Amazon – www.amazon.com
Barnes & Noble – www.bn.com

It's Halloween! - Halloween is a festive holiday celebrated in many parts of the world. The holiday is sometimes serious but mostly fun, full of mystery and magic. It's Halloween is a book the whole family will enjoy, but especially children. Inside, you will find some interesting facts about Halloween, tips for carving the perfect jack-o'-lantern, trick-or-treating safety tips, and information on how the Heimlich Maneuver saves lives. Have fun making quick and easy recipes, craft projects and more. You may want to leave the lights on as you enjoy reading several short stories for kids of all ages. That is, if you're not too scared!

The Magic of Christmas - The Holiday Season usually starts off with Thanksgiving. Then, the mad rush is on for Christmas before bringing in a New Year. Christmas is a festive holiday celebrated in many parts of the world. The holiday is a time for giving as well as receiving. The Magic of Christmas is a book the whole family will enjoy, but especially children. Inside, you will find some interesting facts about Thanksgiving, Christmas, and the New Year. There's information on how the Heimlich Maneuver saves lives. Take a ride by Model Railroading and learn a little about reindeer. Have fun making quick and easy recipes, craft projects and more. You may want to enjoy reading several short stories for kids of all ages as you sit next to your Christmas tree. There's no place like home for the holidays. May all your holidays be merry and bright!

A Precious Gift - A Precious Gift is a collection of short stories about our most cherished treasures, our children. Many people want children, but can't have them. They often become caregivers to others' children. Raising a child can be a long, tedious, and heartbreaking job. Keeping the faith and believing in a higher power, helps bring love, joy and peace to our lives.

Love Storm - Love Storm is a collection of love stories for all occasions. It embraces the romantic in all of us. We want to be with that special person, a lifetime partner, who makes us dizzy with happiness. Sometimes we win at love, and other times we lose. They say that all is fair in love and war, but is it? We have to keep believing that our dreams of the perfect lover will come true. Hopefully, love will come to stay.

Beadweaving - Beadweaving will show you everything you need to know about beads. You can get started making beautiful jewelry and accessories with all kinds of beads. Sell your creations and make money. Beadweaving is full of helpful information about organizing a work space, managing your time, and packaging your jewelry for sale or just to show off. You will be proud of the beautiful, handcrafted jewelry and accessories that's designed and made by you. Start stringing them along!

Mystery Minder - Mystery Minder was written by the "Lady of Mystery" herself. The element of surprise, a nose for news, and a touch of humor, will keep you turning the pages. Are you a sleuth? Can you guess whodunit? Will the villain get their comeuppance? Pull up a chair. You're about to find out!

Rain or Shine - Three Books in One - Short Story Collection. Books include Mystery Minder, Love Storm and A Precious Gift.

Celebration of Love - is a beautiful book of love for all seasons. It's full of entertaining articles, stories and poetry about love. A timeless piece of work by the lady of love herself, it makes for warm-hearted reading no matter how young or young-at heart you may be. Burning with emotion, it will move you if read alone or given as a gift. Open the pages, and give yourself the gift of love!

Spirit Star Rising – Spirit Star Series – Volume 1
Melody Lovell expected summer to be humdrum without her friends and parties to enjoy. Having a bothersome, little brother around was enough to ruin anyone's vacation. The one thing she looked forward to was delving deeper into her beloved music. Melody dreamed of meeting her favorite rock singer one day, but was astonished to discover the famous, Willy B. Bold, practically in her back yard, fishing. They shared a common bond and found they made beautiful music together.

Melody experienced adventure, romance, and fun

enough to last a lifetime, but not without her share of problems. She learned some important lessons about life, growing up, winning over her rivals, facing the ghosts in her closet, and keeping the evil eye at bay. She often called upon the angels and spirits to help her out, but sometimes help came in the most unexpected of ways. She also acquired some family traditions along the way. Making the family's famous recipes and beaded jewelry were a given. Melody also followed in the footsteps of her mother and grandmother and had the gift of psychic intuition and healing. Sometimes, it was a good thing, but not always.

It all happened at her grandparent's quaint, out-of-the-way, lakeside resort in the heart of the Pennsylvania Mountains. Everything was going great until a foolish revelation started a sleuth of fans and reporters on Willy's trail. Since Melody was the cause of all the havoc on Valley View Mountain, she had to do something to help and fast. A little humor, patience, and quick action were necessary to save the day. It didn't hurt to have a spirit star on hand either. Her spirit star, magically transformed into a beautiful love song, became number one on the pop charts. Read it, sing it, live it here!

Spirit Star Falling – Spirit Star Series - Volume 2
Coming Soon!